RHYTHM**CHANGES**SOLOING FOR JAZZ**FLUTE**

The Guide to Chord Tone Soloing on Rhythm Changes For C Instruments

BUSTER**BIRCH**

FUNDAMENTAL**CHANGES**

Rhythm Changes Soloing for Jazz Flute

The Guide to Chord Tone Soloing on Rhythm Changes for C Instruments

Published by **www.fundamental-changes.com**

Buster Birch

Copyright © 2021 Fundamental Changes Ltd.

The moral right of this author has been asserted.

ISBN: 978-1-78933-230-8

Over 13,000 fans on Facebook: **FundamentalChangesInGuitar**

Instagram: **FundamentalChanges**

Cover Image Copyright: Shutterstock – Furtseff

Dedications

Seren's Serenade is dedicated to my beautiful two-year-old niece Seren.

Bowie's Bounce is dedicated to my four-year-old nephew Bowie, who loves to jump on his trampoline.

Jo's Jacuzzi is dedicated to my lovely wife and her favourite place to be.

Atti's Antics is dedicated to my eighteen-month-old nephew Atticus,
who loves to dance whenever he hears music.

All flute tracks performed by Andy Panayi (www.andypanayi.co.uk)

Contents

About the Author

Buster Birch is an award-winning jazz musician and educator from London, UK. He was a professorial member of the jazz faculty at Trinity Laban Conservatoire of music for seven years, where he taught improvisation, musicianship, jazz repertoire and jazz history classes. He has been a visiting lecturer at The Royal Academy of Music, The Guildhall School of Music & Drama and Middlesex University.

He is director of the UK's longest running jazz summer school. Nominated for the All-Party Parliamentary Award for Jazz Education, **www.theoriginalukjazzsummerschool.com** is a week-long residential course hosted at The Royal Welsh College of Music & Drama for singers and all instrumentalists of all ages and experience levels. When the summer school was unable to run in 2020, he set up **www.theonlineukjazzcourse.com**, a three-day online course for singers and instrumentalists featuring simultaneous live masterclasses, workshops and play along sessions with sixteen of the UK's finest jazz educators.

He offers regular online jazz workshops, where he coaches adult learners from all over the world, on all instruments, through classic jazz repertoire. Video recordings of past classes are available on his website.

He is co-founder and course leader for the BYMT Jazz School (**www.bymt.co.uk**) which runs regular jazz improvisation classes for school children at the county music centre. In 2017, BYMT Jazz School won the prestigious Will Michael Diploma Award for Jazz Education – a national award recognising "outstanding commitment to jazz education" and "acknowledging the work of those field practitioners who are actually delivering jazz education and in many cases helping to combat the widespread jazz phobia among classroom music teachers and instrumental tutors."

Buster is also a busy freelance jazz drummer who has worked with many of the UK's finest jazz musicians. He has an honours degree in music from the University of London and a post-graduate diploma in jazz performance from the Guildhall School of Music and Drama. He also studied at the Drummers Collective in New York City and privately with Jim Chapin and Joe Morello (of The Dave Brubeck Quartet).

He has performed at virtually every major concert hall and jazz club in London, as well as major international festivals; he has toured in over thirty countries and recorded over thirty albums. He has been a member of three world music groups with whom he recorded and toured extensively, and has played for world-class orchestras including The Royal Philharmonic Orchestra, and deputised on West End shows.

He created his own critically acclaimed show **www.busterplaysbuster.com** which features the Buster Birch Jazz Quartet playing live and in sync to the screening of Buster Keaton feature-length silent movies, for which he arranged and scored over 4hrs of music.

Buster is a member of the following bands: ARQ (The Alison Rayner Quintet) – winners of the All-Party Parliamentary Award for "Best UK Jazz Ensemble", The Jo Fooks Quartet, Heads South, The London Jazz Trio and The Halstead Jazz Club Big Band.

For more information, please see **www.busterbirch.co.uk**

Introduction

This book isn't about how to play *flute*, it's about how to play *music*. But while the concepts contained here apply to any instrument, the exercises in this edition have been tailored to fit within the flute's unique range.

When starting with jazz improvisation, a common approach is to use a "parent" scale over a sequence of chords. Safe in the knowledge that all of the notes fit, you are free to focus on the improvisation and avoid getting bogged down with thinking too much about the theory. This concept is featured in my *Beginner Jazz Soloing* series of books.

Let's take a look at the standard ii-V-I progression in Bb Major (Cm7 – F7 – Bbmaj7) and see how the parent scale method works over the three different chords in that sequence.

We use numbers to identify the degrees (notes) of the scale and Roman numerals to identify chords. Lower case Roman numerals refer to minor chords and upper case numerals refer to Major chords.

Often, in jazz, we talk about using a scale to play a solo over a chord, but it's more helpful to think of the chords as coming *from* a scale.

For example, we can *extract* a Cmi7 (the ii chord) from the Bb Major scale by starting on the second note of the scale (C) and adding thirds above it: C, Eb, G and Bb.

We can extract an F7 (the V chord) from the Bb Major scale by starting on the fifth note of the scale (F) and adding thirds above it: F, A, C and Eb.

We can extract a BbMaj7 (the I chord) from the Bb Major scale by starting on the first Note (Bb) and adding thirds above it: Bb, D F and A.

Bb   D   F   A   Bbmaj7

1   2   3   4   5   6   7   1   I

These three chords combine to create the important ii-V-I sequence, common to hundreds of jazz standard tunes, and they are all contained within the major scale. This is why you can use that one parent scale to improvise over the whole sequence.

Cmi7   F7   Bbmaj7   Bbmajor

ii   V   I   1   2   3   4   5   6   7   1

While this is a good starting point, there are two problems you encounter when playing the major scale over this whole sequence.

Firstly, not every note in the scale sounds great over every chord. Some notes clash slightly and need careful handling. For instance, the Eb clashes with the D in the BbMaj7 chord, and Bb clashes with the A in the F7 chord. These are referred to as *avoid* notes.

You can use avoid notes as *passing notes* within a phrase (i.e. to briefly move between two good sounding notes), but you wouldn't want to feature them by holding them on, or playing them as the chord changes. However, if you are thinking Bb Major all the time when improvising, you are quite likely to feature the Bb note over the F7 chord.

Secondly, thinking in scales tends to make you play too many stepwise scale movements. Most jazz melodies (solos and tunes) are based around arpeggio shapes. This is particularly true of bebop where the inspiration for improvising comes from the underlying chords and moves away from the original melody.

Above we spelled out the arpeggio notes for each chord in the ii-V-I sequence. Using arpeggios on each chord instead of scales solves both these problems and is called *chord tone soloing*. With practice, and by using the exercises in this book, you will start to embed the sound of the important chord tones into your ears. The more you consciously target them in your practice, the more you will be subconsciously drawn to them in your improvisation.

Chord tone soloing is the next step on from thinking in terms of parent scales. Improvising with the chord tones will give your soloing a solid foundation, both harmonically and melodically. It will help you to really *play the changes* and – with the addition of some simple embellishments – you will learn to solo using sophisticated melodies to achieve a more authentic jazz sound.

Get the Audio

The audio files for this book are available to download for free from **www.fundamental-changes.com.** The link is in the top right-hand corner. Simply select this book title from the drop-down menu and follow the instructions to get the audio.

We recommend that you download the files directly to your computer, not to your tablet, and extract them there before adding them to your media library. You can then put them on your tablet, iPod or burn them to CD. On the download page there is a help PDF and we also provide technical support via the contact form.

www.fundamental-changes.com

Instagram: FundamentalChanges

Chapter One – What are Rhythm Changes?

I Got Rhythm was composed by George and Ira Gershwin for the musical *Girl Crazy,* which opened on Broadway in October 1930. The pit orchestra for the opening night was the Red Nichols' band which included Benny Goodman, Gene Krupa, Jack Teagarden, Glenn Miller and Jimmy Dorsey! The show made a star of Ginger Rogers and gave Ethel Merman her Broadway debut. Legend has it that after seeing the reviews, Gershwin told her never to take a singing lesson!

One of the things that made *I Got Rhythm* so popular with musicians is its harmonic structure. The chord sequence can be altered and substituted to create many new variations, but the overall structure is so simple and well-balanced that it always retains its identity. This means that there are endless different ways to explore this tune without getting bored.

In the 1940s bebop era, the chord changes to *I Got Rhythm* became the basis for many new jazz tunes, where a new melody was written to fit over the sequence. The technical name for this idea is a *contrafact* and there are dozens of famous jazz tunes based on these changes and their many subtle variations.

In the bebop era, the melody was often abandoned as an inspiration for soloing and musicians instead focused on creating solos by using notes from the underlying chord changes. This gave them more freedom and paved the way for a whole new jazz language. *Rhythm Changes* became a rite of passage for bebop players to prove one's soloing skills and were often performed at incredibly fast tempos. If you couldn't play over Rhythm Changes, forget it!

Learning to solo on Rhythm Changes teaches you to solo on many different tunes. Even if you can't play the melody (though you should!), you can still take a solo, which is why tunes based on rhythm changes are so popular at jam sessions.

Studying Rhythm Changes is a must for any aspiring jazz musician and something that highly experienced, professional jazz musicians still consider a work in progress.

Form

The first thing you should check before playing any tune is its *form*. This just means how the structure of the tune is arranged. Think of the form as *zooming out* and looking at a map of the music's structure.

A song's form shows the total length (in bars) of music, and shows how those bars are divided into sections. These sections are given letters to identify them. You're probably familiar with language like "in the A section…" or "repeat the B Section twice".

The form of Rhythm Changes

I Got Rhythm is a 32-bar tune that has a two-bar *tag ending* which repeats at the end of the tune. In the original vocal version, Ethel Merman sings *"Who could ask for anything more? Who could ask for anything more?"* in the tag ending until the song finishes. However, no one wants to improvise over a thirty-four bar form – it just doesn't feel good! So usually jazz musicians don't play the tag on the solos and save it for the head (melody) of the tune.

Therefore, most Rhythm Changes tunes have a thirty-two bar AABA form.

You can see from the diagram below that the eight-bar A section repeats, before the contrasting eight-bar B section enters. The piece finishes by repeating the chord sequence from the A section.

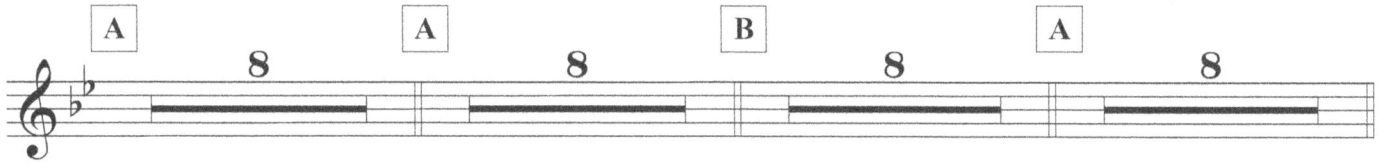

Alternative Changes

Jazz musicians are always looking for new sounds and fresh approaches to old tunes and substituting a chord or two can significantly alter the mood and feeling of a tune. When you change a chord underneath a melody note, you change the musical and emotional relationship between the two. What was a rather bland root or fifth in the melody can suddenly become a soulful ninth or a poignant major seventh, which can give a whole new meaning to a piece.

Nowadays, with so many famous contrafact tunes based on alternative versions of *I Got Rhythm*, the original tune has become less popular – and throughout this book we will cover some common alternative versions of Rhythm Changes which include chord substitutions.

Listen to the first audio track to hear the chord sequence played twice. Follow the chord chart as you listen to the track and take note of where each eight-bar section starts and ends. Repeat this until you can keep your place in the sequence in your head, without needing the chord chart.

Listen out for the D7 chord in bar seventeen, which signals the beginning of the B section, and also for the drum fill in bar 32, which signals the end of the whole sequence.

Example 1a:

You can check out the suggested listening at the end of this book to hear many different versions and contrafacts of Rhythm Changes tunes. It's essential for you to hear the music and start to get inside its structure.

You can access the full Spotify playlist by clicking the link below or by scanning the QR code with your phone

This book is divided into three main sections. Part I covers the A section and introduces the main concepts that you will use to improvise a solo. Part II covers the B section and Part III brings everything together with some sample solos and compositions to play over.

There's a lot of material to get through, so take your time and make sure you are confident on each exercise before moving on.

Part I – The A Section

Chapter Two – First Half of the A Section

The first four bars of the A section feature a two-bar *turnaround* which is repeated. Turnarounds are short sequences of chords that loop back to a starting point. They *turn you around,* back to the beginning of the sequence so it can repeat.

There are many variations of turnarounds, but the one featured here is referred to as a I-vi-ii-V diatonic turnaround. (Diatonic means that all of the notes come from the key signature and no accidentals are required).

Sometimes a BbMaj7 is used for the I chord, but we will be using the more common Bb6, where the major sixth replaces the major seventh.

Example 2a:

Exploring the Chord Tones

When studying any chord sequence, it is a good idea to start by learning the movement of the root notes. Practice playing this sequence of notes until you can hear it in your head and sing it out loud.

Start by playing the root of each chord along with the audio track until you can play it from memory. Then sing along with the audio track. Then sing it without the audio track.

Example 2b:

One of the interesting things about jazz is that there is always an alternative pathway through the chord changes. Even something as simple as playing the root notes in the previous example can be played in different ways. For example, you could take the following path instead.

Example 2c:

When working through the exercises in this book, always think about the alternative pathways you could take through the chord sequence using the same idea.

Now you are going to add some rhythm to Example 2b and turn it into a melodic phrase. In jazz it is common to anticipate a chord by an 1/8th note – particularly chords on the first beat of the bar. This anticipation helps to create forward motion and energy.

Play the following example with the audio track. After the first two bars, the rhythm section repeats the sequence as a backing track for you to improvise your own rhythmic variations. Stick to the same sequence of root notes, just add some anticipation and repetition.

Example 2d:

Now add the fifth of each chord, either above or below, using quarter notes through the sequence. Practice this pattern until you can play it from memory, then try some alternative pathways.

Example 2e:

Let's add some 1/8th note rhythmic *anticipations* to this line to make it a bit more interesting. After the first two bars, the rhythm section repeats the sequence as a backing track for you to improvise your own rhythmic variations.

Example 2f:

Next you are going to include the third of each chord. Now you have more notes than there are places to put them, which means you have to make some choices.

You don't have to play the root on every chord. Often it is not the strongest note to choose because usually the bass is already playing it. When you play a different chord tone you create an interval with the root on the bass and that interval helps to define the harmony.

Example 2g:

Now add some 1/8th note anticipations to this line. After the first two bars, the rhythm section on the audio track repeats the sequence as a backing track for you to improvise your own rhythmic variations.

Example 2h:

Finally, you are going to add the seventh of each chord (the sixth replaces the seventh on the Bb6 chord). With all four chord tones now available there are lots of choices. Notice how much smoother the line can become as you make more chord tones available.

Example 2i:

Once again, apply some 1/8th note anticipations to bring the line to life. After the first two bars, the rhythm section repeats the sequence as a backing track for you to improvise your own rhythmic variations.

Example 2j:

The following example demonstrates the same concept across the first four bars of the A section, which is the I-vi-ii-V turnaround sequence repeated. All four chord tones are available options throughout the sequence and the line is based on a quarter note rhythm with some 1/8th note anticipations.

Example 2k:

The next example demonstrates an alternative line over the same four-bar sequence using the same ingredients.

Example 2l:

Arpeggios

The next stage is to use 1/8th notes to practice arpeggiating the chords. Unlike piano and guitar, wind instruments are designed to play one note at a time. Playing arpeggios means playing the chords one note at a time and offers us a way to outline the harmonic sequence.

Arpeggiating the chord sequence is a great exercise to practice when learning a new tune and something jazz musicians spend a lot of time working on. When playing continuous 1/8th note exercises tongue every up beat and slur onto every down beat.

Because the I-vi-ii-V turnaround sequence has two chords per bar, you have to play 1/8th notes to arpeggiate all four of the chord tones over the space of two beats.

Example 2m:

A common bad habit is to only practice arpeggios in one direction, up from the root. When improvising it is important to be comfortable moving in any direction, therefore you must practice arpeggios in both directions.

Example 2n:

Another common problem is *root bias*. This comes from always practicing scales starting and ending on the root. When you solo, it is important to be comfortable starting and ending on any note of a scale or arpeggio – not just the root.

The following example is a great exercise to practice and combines several skills to help to combat the previously mentioned bad habits.

This 1/8th note line combines arpeggios moving in different directions and starting on different chord tones.

Example 2o:

Bb6 — Gmi7 — Cmi7 — F7

5 3 1 6   b3 1 b3 5   1 b3 1 b7   5 3 5 b7

There are many different pathways you can take through the sequence using this same idea. The following example shows an alternative pathway.

Example 2p:

Bb6 — Gmi7 — Cmi7 — F7

5 6 1 3   b7 5 b3 5   b3 1 b7 5   5 3 5 3

Spend as much time as possible working on this exercise to find new melodic pathways and develop your fluency at different tempos. When practicing arpeggio pathways through chord sequences, try to avoid repeating the same note consecutively as the chord changes.

Now it's time to add the magic ingredient of rhythm and turn those 1/8th note exercises into melodic phrases.

The following examples will teach you a couple of *stock* rhythmic phrases, but as with all of the exercises in this book, these are just a small sample to demonstrate the concept. You should also develop your own ideas and a great way to do this is to steal rhythms you like off your favourite recordings.

Start by clapping the rhythm along with the audio track. Do this until you can hear the whole phrase in your head and process it as one complete unit.

Example 2q:

Now do the same with this alternative stock rhythmic phrase.

Example 2r:

The next part of the process I refer to as *painting by numbers.* You are simply going to apply the rhythmic phrases to arpeggio lines to generate some melodic phrases. They will not be the hippest sounding melodies you've ever heard, but don't worry about that for now. Focus on the process. This is a steppingstone between the melodic exercises and learning to improvise freely. With the tweaks and embellishments that you'll learn later, these basic phrases will become the foundation of some great solos.

Applying the stock rhythm of Example 2q to the arpeggio exercise Example 2o creates this melodic phrase.

Example 2s:

Applying the stock rhythm of Example 2r to the arpeggio exercise Example 2p generates this melodic phrase.

Example 2t:

Bolting two-bar phrases together is an easy way to create a four-bar line. The two 1/8th notes at the beginning of the third bar have been transposed up an octave to allow a smoother connection to the final 1/8th note of the second bar.

Example 2u:

5   3 1 6 b3 1   5   1 b3 1 b7 5 3   b7   5 6   3 b7 5 b3 5   b3 1   5 5   3 5 3

This next example demonstrates an alternative four-bar line using the same ingredients.

Example 2v:

5 6   3 b3 1   5   1 b3 1 b7 5 3   b7 5   3 1 6 b7   5 b3 5   b3 1   5 5 3   b7

Now take some time to explore this concept further and generate more four-bar lines over this sequence using combinations of your own rhythmic phrases and arpeggio pathways.

Voice Leading

Voice leading is a way of thinking *horizontally* through the chords (melody), as opposed to thinking *vertically* (harmonically) up and down the chords – which you do when playing arpeggios. Instead of playing all of the chord tones for every chord, you pick one then move to the nearest note in the next chord.

When there are two chords per bar and the tempo is fast, voice leading is a great way to de-clutter your solo! Memorising a voice leading line through a chord sequence significantly reduces the amount of musical theory you have to process in real time.

A voice leading can use any chord tone (including extensions such as 9s, 11s and 13s), but you are going to stick to 1, 3, 5 and 7 for now.

Starting on the third of the first chord, play through the sequence and switch to the nearest chord tone in the next chord as it changes. If the same note is also in the next chord, then repeat it. Notice how flat the line is.

Example 2w:

Now apply some rhythm to this line. After the first two bars, the rhythm section repeats the sequence as a backing track for you to improvise your own rhythmic variations of this voice leading.

Example 2x:

The repetition of pitch and generally static nature of voice leading can feel strange at first, especially if played solo, with no backing track. However, you must bear in mind that as you repeat the same note the chord underneath it changes. The interval you create with the bass is new on each chord and the feeling of "shifting sand" underneath your static melody line can be very effective.

If you have ever played second or third harmony parts in a big band or brass band, then you will have experienced a similar feeling. Practicing the part alone at home can sound rather uninspiring, but when you rehearse with the band and play that part in the full arrangement it sounds great!

Start with a different chord tone and follow the same rule to create a new horizontal pathway through the sequence.

Example 2y:

Now apply some rhythm to this line. After the first two bars, the rhythm section repeats for you to improvise your own variations.

Example 2z:

Take some time to explore other voice leading pathways you can find by starting from other chord tones. If you stick strictly to the rule of only using the nearest note, you will notice that the lines tend to descend and there are a limited number of pathways.

Now let's add another step. If you also include the *next nearest* chord tone, this will open up many more possible pathways, including ascending lines like this one below.

Example 2z1:

Let's add some rhythm to this line. After the first two bars, the rhythm section repeats the sequence as a backing track for you to improvise your own rhythmic variations.

Example 2z2:

Let's add a bit of magic! You are going to embellish the voice leading melody with the root of each chord. Bouncing between the root notes and the voice leading melody is a simple and effective way to generate strong melodic phrases over the sequence and turn a simple exercise into something that sounds good in a solo. The following example uses root notes to embellish Example 2z.

Example 2z3:

As before, bolting together two-bar phrases is an easy way to create a four-bar line. The following example combines Example 2z2 and Example 2z with the addition of root notes to embellish the line.

Example 2z4:

This next example demonstrates an alternative four-bar line using the same concepts.

Example 2z5:

VI Instead of vi

A common alteration to the turnaround sequence is to replace the Gmi7 (vi) with G7 (VI). This works because G7 is the dominant seventh (V7) of the Cmi7 chord that follows, but it means that you are using *chromatic* harmony, so you have to take into account the B natural in the G7 chord as this was a Bb in the original Gm7 chord.

Example 2z6:

Reharmonizing the minor chord vi with the alternative major chord VI gives the music a brighter sound and this version of the turnaround was particularly favoured by the bebop players.

All of the previous exercises should also be practiced with the I-VI-ii-V alteration.

The following example demonstrates the arpeggio line from Example 2v adapted to fit the new I-VI-ii-V sequence. Look out for the B natural on the G7 chords.

Example 2z7:

The following example demonstrates the voice leading line from Example 2z5 adapted to fit the new I-VI-ii-V sequence.

Example 2z8:

Chapter Three – Second Half of the A Section

There are a few variations to deal with in this section of the Rhythm Changes, so we'll break it down and work on two bars at a time.

The chords for bars 5-6 vary from tune to tune and there are three common choices that you will encounter.

In version one, the Ab7 (bVII7) is sometimes referred to as a *back door* dominant and resolves up a tone to the tonic.

Example 3a:

In version two the sequence adds a first inversion of Bb7 in bar five and a diminished chord substitution in bar six. You will learn more about these in Chapter Five, so don't panic if this sounds like a foreign language to you right now!

Example 3b:

In version three, the shift in bar six from the major IV chord (the 3rd is a G note) to the minor iv chord (the 3rd is Gb) creates the same *inner part* movement as version one, where the third from the Eb7 (G) moves to the flat seven of the Ab7 chord (Gb).

Example 3c:

This is a particularly good descending voice leading movement that is often used on version one (shown here) and version three.

Example 3d:

Now add some rhythmic phrasing and root note embellishments to turn that voice leading into a melodic phrase.

Example 3e:

The diminished chord in version two helps to create a great ascending voice leading in the bass, which will probably sound familiar to you.

Example 3f:

Now give it some rhythmic phrasing and root note embellishments to turn that voice leading into a melodic phrase.

Example 3g:

As you can see, voice leadings work well on all versions of bars 5-6, but you can use the arpeggio method too. Practice an 1/8th note arpeggio pathway through version one.

Example 3h:

Apply the stock rhythm from Exercise 2q to generate a melodic phrase.

Example 3i:

Now practice an 1/8th note arpeggio pathway through version two.

Example 3j:

Apply the stock rhythm from Exercise 2r to generate a melodic phrase.

Example 3k:

Here's an 1/8th note arpeggio pathway through version three.

Example 3l:

Use the stock rhythm from Exercise 2q to generate a melodic phrase.

Example 3m:

There are two different versions of bars 7-8 of the A section. To understand why you need to look back at the form.

As discussed in Chapter One, the form of rhythm changes is AABA

Let's label the three A sections A1, A2 and A3.

A1 and A3 are followed by another A section, but A2 is followed by the new B section.

The chords in bars 7-8 of A1 and A3 contain a turnaround because the harmony needs bring you back to the start of an A section. The F7 leads smoothly to the Bb6 in bar one.

Example 3n:

In A2, the final bar doesn't loop to the beginning of an A section, instead it resolves to the home Bb6. It doesn't need to contain the F7 chord because the following B section heads off in a new key centre.

Example 3o:

You can start to see how we've ended up with so many different variations on Rhythm Changes!

At this point it may start to feel a bit overwhelming, but don't worry! I'll be covering some of the different versions of Rhythm Changes you may encounter later. However, it's important to note that even if you only know a melodic route around one set of changes, this will normally sound pretty good whatever the chords are doing underneath because they're all strongly related.

The following examples combine the techniques you have learnt over different versions of the second half of the A section.

This line over A1 uses voice leading on version three of bars 5-6 (adapted from Example 3e) and an arpeggio phrase on the turnaround in bars 7-8 (adapted from Example 2s).

Example 3p:

This line over A1 uses voice leading on version two of bars 5-6 (Example 3g) and voice leading on the turnaround in bars 7-8 (Example 2z3).

Example 3q:

This line over A2 uses an arpeggio phrase on version one of bars 5-6 (Example 3i) and an arpeggio phrase on the resolution in bars 7-8.

Example 3r:

This line over A2 uses an arpeggio phrase on version two of bars 5-6 (Example 3k) and voice leading on the resolution in bars 7-8.

Example 3s:

Chapter Four – Joining the Dots

In this chapter you are going to learn four techniques to embellish the arpeggio pathways and give your melodic phrases a more authentic bebop / jazz flavour. These techniques can be used as a way of connecting different arpeggios as you move from chord to chord, *targeting* chord tones and introducing some chromaticism.

Chromatic Passing Notes

A chromatic passing note can be used to fill a one tone gap between arpeggios.

Example 4a:

Let's add some rhythm to this arpeggio exercise to help it become a melodic phrase.

Example 4b:

Scale Tone Passing Notes

A scale tone can be used to fill the gap between arpeggios. The scale tone comes from the chord sequence's parent scale, which for this turnaround sequence is Bb Major.

Example 4c:

Again, add some interesting rhythms to this arpeggio exercise to turn it into a melodic phrase.

Example 4d:

Chromatic Approach Notes

Any chord tone can be approached by a note a semi-tone above or below it.

Example 4e:

Here's a rhythmic idea that turns this arpeggio exercise into a melodic phrase.

Example 4f:

Enclosures

An enclosure extends the approach note idea by using two approach notes, one above and one below. The approach notes can be scale tones or chromatic notes. The tension created by playing either side of the note is resolved by landing on the chord tone, thus highlighting it. Think of it as a sandwich, where the approach notes are the bread and the chord tone is the filling.

Any combination of scale tones or chromatic notes, above or below, is acceptable, but a common pattern is to play a scale tone above followed by a semi-tone below, landing on the target chord tone.

Example 4g:

1	3	EA	EB	1	b7	5	b3	1	b3	EA	EB	1	b7	5	3

Once again, use rhythm to turn this arpeggio exercise into a melodic phrase.

Example 4h:

1	EA	EB	1	b7	b3	1	EA	EB	1	b7

So far, you have used the embellishment techniques at the end of an arpeggio idea to connect the chords together. But all of these techniques can be used *within* an arpeggio, or at the start of an arpeggio, to create a limitless supply of variations to your line.

The next few examples demonstrate how you can apply these new techniques to the first and second half of the A section. Take some time to explore these techniques further and come up with your own examples.

This line over the first half of the A section uses chromatic passing notes, an enclosure, and chromatic approach notes.

Example 4i:

5	3	1	6	b3	1	5	1	CPN	b7	5	1	CPN	b7	EA	EB	5	3	b3	1	CAN	1	b3	1	CAN 3 1

This line over the second half of A1 uses a scale tone passing note, a chromatic approach note, a chromatic passing note, and an enclosure.

Example 4j:

This line over the second half of A2 uses enclosures and a chromatic approach note.

Example 4k:

Chapter Five – A Section Chord Substitutions

It is common for jazz musicians to *reharmonize* a tune by substituting one chord for another. Substitutions normally create a smoother movement between chords and can add some chromatic harmony to spice things up a bit.

Groups of chords can also be substituted and sometimes there's even an *alternative* set of chord changes for a whole tune. Check out Miles Davis' recording of *Stella By Starlight* on *'58 Sessions*. Then listen to John Coltrane's recording of *Body and Soul* on *Coltrane's Sound* (1964). What do you think of their chord choices?

Jazz musicians often play alternative substitutions on the fly behind a soloist and may play different chords from one chorus to the next. However, doing this in a jam session with inexperienced musicians is probably not a good idea. It is asking a lot of them and may not enhance the overall experience for the audience! However, adding substitutions to a chord chart that the whole band plays, or practicing through some pre-agreed alternative changes with your bandmates, is a good way to work on these ideas.

This chapter will cover three of the most common chord substitutions found in Rhythm Changes. You will learn why they work and how to incorporate them into your soloing.

Substituting iii for I

When you're playing jazz, it is safe to assume that the bassist will play the root note of the chord. Having the root already covered allows the pianist or guitarist to use *rootless voicings* that build chords up from the third or fifth and add extensions.

In jazz, it's common to substitute the I chord with the iii chord. For example, instead of playing Bb6, we can play Dmi7 instead. Let's see what happens when we do this.

Imagine that the bass player is still playing the original root note Bb. The notes of Dmi7 are D F A C. As intervals over the Bb bass note these are 3, 5, 7 and 9. Substituting Dmi7 for BbMaj7 creates a BbMaj9 chord sound.

Example 5a:

Chord iii is often used as a substitution for chord I in the third bar of the A section of Rhythm Changes. This substitution works well with the VI (G7) instead of vi (Gmi7) chord as it creates another *auxiliary* ii-V within the sequence. Play through the arpeggios to learn the chord tones of this new sequence.

This line includes the iii for I substitution in the third bar.

Example 5b:

Bb6 — G7 | Cmi7 — F7 | Dmi7 — G7 | Cmi7 — F7

1 3 5 3 3 1 3 5 b3 1 b7 5 1 3 5 b7 1 b7 5 b3 1 3 5 b7 b3 1 b7 1 b7 5 3 1

Here's an idea based on those arpeggios with some added rhythmic phrasing.

Example 5c:

Bb6 — G7 | Cmi7 — F7 | Dmi7 — G7 | Cmi7 — F7

3 5 CAN 3 1   5   b3 1 EA EB 1   5 b7   1 b7 5 CPN 1   3   5   b3 1 b7 CPN 5 3 1

Sometimes chord iii is also used instead of chord I in the first bar of the sequence. This line uses the iii for I substitution both times.

Example 5d:

Dmi7 — G7 | Cmi7 — F7 | Dmi7 — G7 | Cmi7 — F7

b7 5 b3 1 1 3   b7   b3 1 b7 CAN 3 1 b7   1   b3 5 b7 3 1   3   1 b7 5 CPN 1 3 b7

Diminished Chord Substitutions

By playing a diminished chord on the *third* of a dominant 7 we can create a rootless V7b9 chord.

For example, instead of playing G7, we can play B Diminished 7. Let's see what happens when we do this.

Imagine that the bass player is still playing the original root note G. The notes of B Diminished are B D F Ab. As intervals over the G bass note these are 3, 5, 7 and b9. So, substituting B Diminished 7 for G7 creates a G7b9 chord. This chord adds a bit of harmonic tension to the G7 chord. It makes the chord sequence more interesting and allows you to access some new notes to solo with.

Example 5e:

B diminished can substitute for the G7 in the I-VI-ii-V version of the turnaround. As you can see, diminished substitutions create a smooth bassline, ascending in semi-tones. Play the arpeggios to learn the chord tones of this new sequence.

Example 5f:

This rhythmic line contains the dim7 substitution for chord VI both times.

Example 5g:

When substituting chord iii (Dmi7) for chord I (Bb6) in bar three, as shown earlier, you can approach it with a C# Diminished 7 chord, which is a substitute for A7b9, the V7 of Dmin7.

Example 5h:

Using both diminished chord substitutions creates a chromatically ascending bassline through the first five chords. Play the arpeggios to learn the chord tones of this new sequence.

Example 5i:

Bb6   B dim7   C mi7   C#dim7   D mi7   G 7   C mi7   F 7

3 1 6 1   1 b3 b5 dim7   5 b3 1 b7 1 b3 b5 dim7   5 b3 1 b7 3 5 b7 1   b3 1 b7 5 1 3 5 3

This line includes the additional dim7 substitution with some fun rhythmic phrasing to create a jazz melody.

Example 5j:

Bb6   B dim7   C mi7   C#dim7   D mi7   G 7   C mi7   F 7

3 1   b3 1   b3 1   b3 1   b3 1 CAN 1 b7 5   3   1 b3 EA EB 1 b7 5

Tritone Substitutions

A tritone is a dissonant sounding three tone interval. All dominant seventh chords have a tritone interval between the major third and flattened seventh.

There are always two dominant seventh chords that share the same tritone between their third and seventh and they are always a flat five (b5 or tritone) interval apart

Example 5k:

F 7   B 7

The above dominant seventh chords can be substituted for each other because their thirds and sevenths are the same pitch. The third of F7 is A and the seventh of B7 is A. The seventh of F7 is Eb and the third of B7 is D#.

Another way to remember a tritone substitution is to think of the root of each chord. They are a tritone (b5) apart.

Instead of F7 you can use B7, and instead of B7 you can use F7. Like everything else, this concept works in all 12 keys.

In the first half of the A section we can substitute the F7 with B7, giving a smooth, chromatic movement between the Cmi7 (ii) and the Bb6 (I).

Play through the sequence with the tritone substitutions to learn the chord tones.

Example 5l:

This melodic line includes the tritone substitutions.

Example 5m:

As discussed in Chapter Two, the major VI can replace the minor vi chord in the first half of the A section. This G7 chord can then be substituted with its tritone substitution Db7 to create another alternative sequence. Play the arpeggios to learn the chord tones.

Example 5n:

This melodic line includes the Db7 tritone substitution of the VI7 (G7) chord.

Example 5o:

Combining Substitutions

All three of the chord substitutions you have learnt in this chapter can be combined in the chord sequence. The following examples show a few possible variations, but you should also explore your own.

The next example combines all these substitution ideas:

- The VI for vi (G7 in place of Gm)

- The diminished substitution (C#7b9) for the V chord (A7b9)

- This leads to the Dmi7 chord, which is the iii for I substitution

- Then two tritone substitutions, Db7 and B7, create a chromatically descending bassline at the end.

Play the arpeggios to learn the chord tones of this new sequence.

Example 5p:

This line, over the same sequence, includes one chromatic passing note, but mainly consists of chord tones.

Example 5q:

The next example includes two diminished substitutions in the first half, which create a chromatic ascending bassline all the way to the iii for I substitution (Dmi7) in the third bar. Play the arpeggios to learn the chord tones of this sequence.

Example 5r:

This line, over the same sequence, includes an enclosure and two chromatic passing notes.

Example 5s:

Chapter Six – Soloing Over the Whole A Section

So far, you have worked with two- and four-bar segments of music. Now it is time to play over a complete eight-bar A section. At first this can seem daunting, but after working through the ideas so far you already have clear strategies in place for the various segments, so let's start by bolting them together.

Remember, there are two different endings to the A section. A1 and A3 both end with the turnaround, whereas A2 resolves to the I chord.

This example over A1 combines examples 2z5 and 3p, with the addition of a few embellishments.

Example 6a:

This example over A1 combines the chromatic passing note (Example 4b) and the enclosure (Example 4h) with the voice leading examples 3g and 2z3.

Example 6b:

This example over A2 combines the diminished chord substitutions (Exercise 5j) with the arpeggio and voice leading examples 3k and the second half of 3s.

Example 6c:

One simple strategy to make your solo sound more cohesive is to use *question and answer* phrasing. The key to this is in the rhythm. If you play an identical or similar rhythm for both phrases, they will sound like they belong together as one complete musical sentence.

This next example uses a combination of the embellished arpeggio ideas that you learnt in Chapter Four. Notice how the use of very similar rhythmic phrasing ties the two lines together and makes them sound like one complete idea.

Example 6d:

Another useful strategy to build excitement throughout your solo is to increase the rhythmic density. Notice how this eight-bar line builds in activity. There are more rests at the beginning and more notes at the end.

Example 6e:

Another common way to build intensity through your solo is to simply start low and end high. Notice how this eight-bar phrase increases in pitch throughout.

Example 6f:

At a quick tempo, voice leading ideas can be a life saver! Instead of having to mentally process all of those chord tones as they fly past, it can be much easier to memorise a good voice leading pathway that you know works well over the whole sequence. Applying some simple rhythmic riffs to the voice leading sounds great at fast tempos.

Illinois Jacquet was the master of this approach. Check out his recording of *Lester Leaps In* on the album *Desert Winds*.

Example 6g:

Part II – The B Section

Chapter Seven – The Bridge

Let's move on to study the chords on the bridge of Rhythm Changes.

There are some key features of this eight-bar section to consider.

1. The chords are all the same *type* of chord (Dominant 7).

2. The root movement moves in fourths.

3. The sequence features chromatic harmony, which means the chords contain notes that are not in the key signature of Bb Major.

4. Each chord lasts for two bars, so the harmony is relatively *static* when compared to the two-chords-per-bar phrasing of the A section.

Start by playing through the arpeggios to learn the chord tones.

Example 7a:

Now let's take the four key features listed above and explore how they can be used to help us create great solos.

Having four chords that are all the same *type* in this sequence makes it easier to use *motivic* improvisation. This is when you take a short melodic idea or *motif* and repeat its shape throughout the sequence, but adjust the pitches to fit each new chord.

Let's demonstrate this on D7 with a two-bar phrase that you learnt in Chapter Four.

Example 7b:

EA EB 1 3   1 CPN b7 1 5 CAN 3

The numbers under each note relate to the interval played on each chord.

EA = Enclosure Above

EB = Enclosure Below

CAN = Chromatic Approach Note

CPN = Chromatic Passing Note

STPN = Scale Tone Passing Note

Now transpose the phrase to fit the next chord in the sequence (G7). Notice how the intervals you play don't change, but the pitches are different.

Example 7c:

EA EB 1 3   1 CPN b7 1 5 CAN 3

This new chord is a fourth away from the previous chord, but it is the same *type* of chord. Therefore, if you transpose the phrase by a fourth, all of the notes have the same relationship to the new chord.

Let's take this motivic idea and play it through the whole sequence. All of the chords are a fourth apart and follow the *cycle of fourths* around to F7. Everything leads to that final V7 chord which smoothly brings us back to the I chord (Bb) at the start of the final A section.

Example 7d:

EA EB 1 3   1 CPN b7 1 5 CAN 3   EA EB 1 3   1 CPN b7 1 5 CAN 3

Transposing the exact same phrase through the whole eight-bar sequence is challenging, but a good exercise to practise. It will help you develop control over your playing and clarity in your thinking. However, when you are soloing it can sound more musical if you include a few variations as you repeat the idea. These could be variations in the rhythm, melodic embellishments and extending or contracting the phrase. For example:

Example 7e:

A variation on this concept is to play a longer line over the first four bars, then repeat that idea down a tone to fit the last four bars. That is exactly what Gershwin did in the original melody!

Example 7f:

Chromatic Harmony on the Bridge

Let's take a moment to explore the chromatic harmony on the bridge. The first three chords include notes that are not in the original Bb key signature. The D7 includes an F#, the G7 includes a B natural, and the C7 includes an E natural.

All these notes are the major thirds of the chords. Thirds are always a good choice to target when trying to outline the harmony, but the thirds in this sequence are particularly strong because they do not belong to the original key signature, so they really stand out.

This next line uses the previous idea of repeating a four-bar line down a tone, but features the major thirds at the beginning of each chord change.

Example 7g:

Reharmonizing the Bridge

Just like the A section, we can reharmonize the B section. There are fundamentally three different ways to reharmonize the bridge:

1. Substitute one chord for another

2. Use fewer chords

3. Add more chords

If the harmony is static, we can add chords to create more harmonic movement. For example, any V7 chord can have its related ii chord added before it. Adding the ii chord of each V7 is one way to create more harmonic movement on the bridge, as in Example 7h.

Play through the arpeggios to the learn the new chord sequence, which adds the ii in front of each V7 chord. Notice how each chord becomes the next minor 7 chord by flattening it's third.

Example 7h:

This line uses the idea of repeating a four-bar phrase down a tone, but now includes the added ii chords.

Example 7i:

Here's another line that uses voice leading to feature the shift between the major and minor thirds.

Example 7j:

The tritone substitution you learnt in Chapter Five is often used to create alternative chord sequences on the bridge of Rhythm Changes. Applying a tritone substitution to the second and fourth chord creates this chromatically descending sequence.

Play through the arpeggios to learn the chord tones.

Example 7k:

3 1 b7 5   1 5 b7 1   3 1 b7 5   1 3 1 b7   3 1 b7 5   1 5 b7 1   3 1 b7 5   1 3 1 5

This line hits the major thirds of each chord to highlight this alternative sequence.

Example 7l:

3 STPN 1 3 EA EB 5   1 CPN b7 3   3   3   b7 1 5 CAN 3 3   3

STPN 1 EA EB 5   3 1 CPN b7   3   b7 CPN 1 5   3 1 b7

Now add the related ii chords to each V7 chord in this new sequence. Play through the arpeggios to learn the chord tones.

Example 7m:

5 b3 1 b7   3 5 b7 1   5 b3 1 b7   3 5 b7 5   1 b3 5 b7   3 1 b7 5   1 b3 5 b7   3 1 b7 5

This line uses voice leading through the new sequence.

Example 7n:

This alternative sequence uses tritone substitutions on the first and third chords to land on the original F7 chord. Play through the arpeggios to learn the chord tones.

Example 7o:

This line features enclosures to embellish the chord tones.

Example 7p:

Again, you can add the related ii chords to the previous sequence, to generate more harmonic movement. Play through the arpeggios to learn the chord tones.

Example 7q:

This line uses voice leading to feature the descending thirds.

Example 7r:

As you can see, using a few reharmonization techniques can generate an abundance of new chord changes that fit over the original sequence, and provide a rich source of harmonic material for jazz musicians to mine night after night.

Finally, check out this bridge sequence from the famous Sonny Stitt tune *Eternal Triangle*. He extends the tritone substitutions further back around the cycle and then catches up by doubling the harmonic pace in the second half of the sequence, taking you around all 12 points on the cycle of fourths!

Example 7s:

Here's a line over the bridge of *Eternal Triangle*. It starts with embellished chord tones, then uses voice leading on the second half when the chords are flying past!

Example 7t:

The previous two ideas go way beyond what we've covered so far, but I wanted to give you an insight into where it's possible to take the music with just a few interesting substitution ideas.

Part III – Bringing It All Together

Chapter Eight – Sample Solos

Now you've worked on all of the separate segments of Rhythm Changes it is time to play over a complete thirty-two-bar chorus. This can seem like a lot of space to fill, but you are not starting from scratch. You already have clear strategies in place for the different segments, so start by bolting them together.

In this first solo:

- A1 is taken from Example 6e

- A2 is taken from Example 6c

- The B section is Example 7g

- A3 is taken from Example 6f

This method may not create the most musical sounding solo, but it is a good exercise to help you deal with the form of the tune and think about the bigger picture. We're still focused on the process of learning to solo on the whole form, not performing ground breaking music right now!

As you play through the solo, think about the techniques that are being used.

- Are you playing a voice leading movement or an arpeggio line?

- What embellishment techniques are added?

- Can you spot any question and answer phrases or motivic repetition of ideas?

After you've worked through this idea, try bolting together different examples in your own solos to help you learn to play the complete form. You can play any idea in any order, so the possibilities are endless! Once you're confident you can vary and embellish my ideas as much as you want to create solos that are a little more personal to you.

Example 8a:

The next example uses all new material and has been written as a complete solo, rather than bolting together sections. Notice how similar rhythmic and motivic ideas are used throughout to tie the melody together.

A common mistake that less experienced improvisers make is to introduce too many new ideas too quickly. Repeating and reworking your ideas over a chorus gives the listener something to grab onto and makes your solo more interesting.

Example 8b:

Chapter Nine – Compositions

Different styles of Rhythm Changes have emerged as jazz has evolved over the decades. I have written four *pastiche* compositions to demonstrate some of the more common types of Rhythm Changes. Throughout, I have used the elements you have studied in this book to create these tunes, as well as adding a few stylistic touches.

Each tune includes a full backing track with one head, two choruses for improvising over, and one head to finish. I have also provided separate practice tracks for each section of each tune to help you prepare. I suggest you spend a bit of time practising improvising over each eight-bar section separately and get a strategy together, before attempting the whole thirty-two bar sequence.

Seren's Serenade

The opening statement of this tune is based on the original *I Got Rhythm* phrase and the melody utilises a question and answer structure throughout. The A sections have a two feel in the rhythm section, which changes to a four feel on the bridge, to give the tune a lift.

Before attempting the whole piece, practice improvising over each eight-bar section separately, using the backing tracks in the audio download.

Example 9a:

Example 9b:

Example 9c:

Example 9d:

Bowie's Bounce

This tune was inspired by the old swing classic *Christopher Columbus* and uses a simple riff that follows a voice leading idea moving in contrary (opposite) motion to the bassline. The turnaround in bars 1-4 is a repeat of the chromatic sequence found in bars 5-6 of the alternative Rhythm Changes. The bridge uses two tritone substitutions to create a chromatically descending sequence and the addition of the #11 extensions give a modern twist to contrast with the early swing feel of the A sections.

Before attempting the whole piece, practice improvising over each eight-bar section separately with the backing tracks.

Example 9e:

Example 9f:

Example 9g:

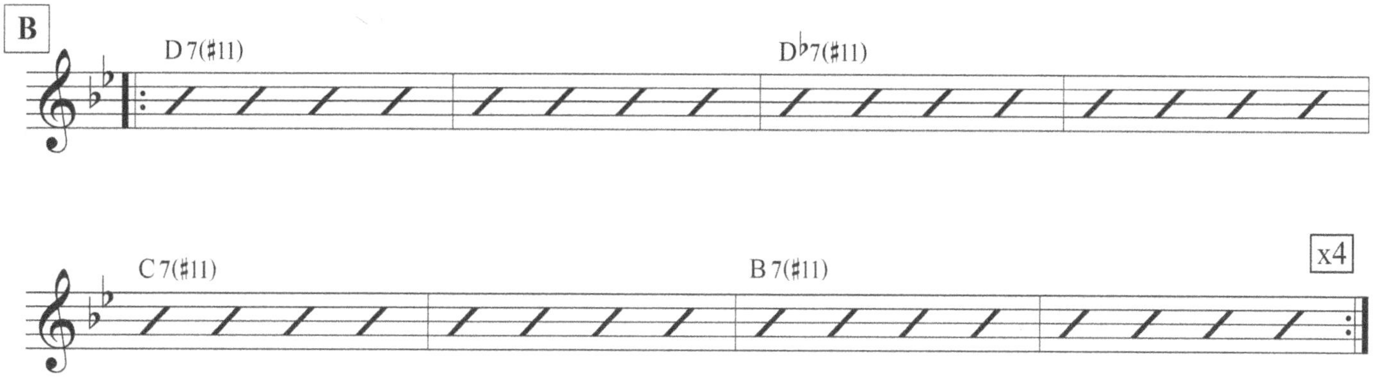

Example 9h:

A1
B♭6 B♭7/D E♭7 E dim7 B♭6 B♭7/D E♭7 E dim7
B♭6 B♭7/D E♭7 E dim7 B♭ F 7
A2
B♭6 B♭7/D E♭7 E dim7 B♭6 B♭7/D E♭7 E dim7
B♭6 B♭7/D E♭7 E dim7 B♭
B
D 7(♯11) D♭7(♯11)
C 7(♯11) B 7(♯11)
A3
B♭6 B♭7/D E♭7 E dim7 B♭6 B♭7/D E♭7 E dim7
B♭6 B♭7/D E♭7 E dim7 B♭

Jo's Jacuzzi

This tune is written in the style of a Charlie Parker Rhythm Changes, such as *Anthropology*, and incorporates some bebop language and phrasing. When learning a tune like this, break it down into separate phrases and work on each one slowly until you can play the rhythm and articulation correctly. Then gradually bolt the phrases together until you can play the whole piece.

Before attempting the whole piece, practice improvising over each eight-bar section separately with the backing tracks.

Example 9i:

Example 9j:

Example 9k:

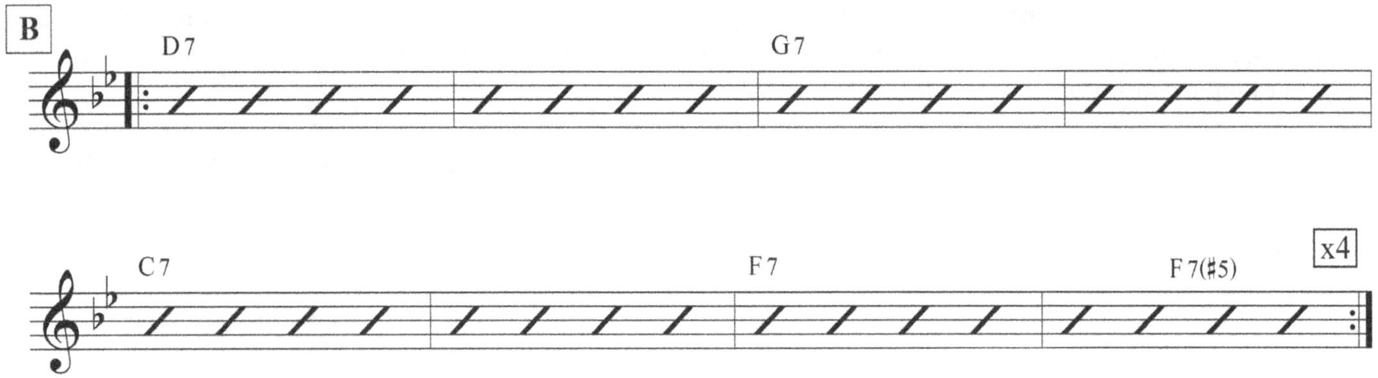

Example 9l:

Atti's Antics

This tune has a calypso groove and was inspired by the classic Blue Mitchell tune *Fungii Mama*. Sonny Rollins was one of the first jazz musicians to fuse calypso music with jazz on his famous recording of *St. Thomas*. Since then, many other jazz musicians have explored the joyful feeling of improvising over this dance rhythm.

Before attempting the whole piece, practice improvising over each eight-bar section separately with the backing tracks.

Example 9m:

Example 9n:

Example 9o:

Conclusion

You have covered a lot of material in this book and learned to "batch process" the busy chord sequences of Rhythm Changes, which is the only way to deal with so much information at speed. With practice, your brain will get more used to processing several bars of music as a single unit, allowing you to *zoom out* and see the bigger picture.

You have also learned the importance of working on each section separately and doing the preparation before putting it all together. So, if necessary, go back and work on the sections that you are not so fluent with. So much of your playing on busy changes has to be automatic. It is not possible to be creative and improvise if, at the same time, you are trying to think about the *maths* of the music. You have to be free of that.

As the great Charlie Parker said, "Practice, practice, practice. Then when you get up on that bandstand, forget all that and just play." Well, he didn't quite put it like that, but you get the idea! Charlie Parker practised for thirteen hours a day, every day, for four years. In doing so, he automated a lot of his thinking and melodic pathways through the music to create a solid form that he could vary and embellish with ease.

Good luck!

Buster Birch

Get Your Free Practice Resources

This book has covered some essential concepts and techniques required for jazz improvisation, based on teaching methods I use in my jazz workshops (**www.busterbirch.co.uk/onlinejazzworkshops**). I hope you enjoyed developing these skills and that your knowledge and confidence has increased to the point where you feel comfortable improvising and creating your own music.

Learning to improvise and play jazz is a lifelong pursuit. It takes a lot of work, but can be rewarding. The more you practice, the more you will improve. The more you study, the more you will understand and appreciate this great art form. You never *get there*. The secret is to get the most out of the journey.

You can reach me through my Facebook page **www.facebook.com/BusterBirchPublic** or my website **www.busterbirch.co.uk** where you can join my mailing list and receive a free digital book, practice resources and updates on future publications.

Best wishes and thank you.

Buster

Suggested Listening

The following recordings of *I Got Rhythm* are available on a specially created Spotify playlist. You can scan the QR code with your phone to jump straight to it.

Recordings of I Got Rhythm

Ethel Merman – Compilation: *Classic Years of Ethel Merman*

Red Nichols & His Five Pennies – Compilation: *Red Nichols in Chronology* (1930)

Louis Armstrong and his Orchestra – OKeh Records (1931)

Interview with George Gershwin – *Variations on I Got Rhythm* (1934)

Stephane Grappelli and Django Reinhardt – *Swing From Paris* (1935)

Benny Goodman – *Carnegie Hall Jazz Concert* (1938)

Art Tatum – *Art Tatum's Finest Hour* (1940)

Charlie Parker, Coleman Hawkins, Lester Young – *Jazz at the Philharmonic vol 14* (1946)

Nat King Cole Trio – Compilation: *Transcriptions* (1949)

Count Basie and his Orchestra – Compilation: *America's #1 Band* (1950)

Oscar Peterson – *Just a Memory* (1951)

Hampton Hawes – *Hampton Hawes Trio vol 1* (1955)

Mark Murphy – *Let Yourself Go* (1957)

Ella Fitzgerald – *Ella Fitzgerald Sings the George and Ira Gershwin Song Book* (1959)

Lena Horne & The Marty Paich Orchestra – *Lena… Lovely and Alive* (1962)

Sarah Vaughan – *Sweet 'n' Sassy* (1964)

Zoot Sims – *Zoot Sims and the Gershwin Brothers* (1975)

Popular Contrafacts on Rhythm Changes

52nd Street Theme – Thelonious Monk (1944)

Anthropology – Charlie Parker (1946)

The Bridge – Sonny Rollins (1962)

Chasin' The Bird – Charlie Parker (1947)

Constellation – Charlie Parker (1948)

Cottontail – Duke Ellington (1940)

Crazeology – Benny Harris (1947)

Dexterity – Charlie Parker (1947)

The Eternal Triangle – Sonny Stitt (1957)

Fungii Mama – Blue Mitchell (1964)

Good Bait – Tadd Dameron (1944)

Kim – Charlie Parker (1952)

Lester Leaps In – Lester Young (1939)

Moose The Mooche – Charlie Parker (1946)

Oleo – Sonny Rollins (1954)

An Oscar For Treadwell – Charlie Parker (1950)

Passport – Charlie Parker (1949)

Red Cross – Charlie Parker (1945)

Rhythm-A-Ning – Thelonious Monk (1958)

Salt Peanuts – Dizzy Gillespie (1942)

Second Balcony Jump – Jerry Valentine (1946)

The Serpent's Tooth – Miles Davis (1953)

Shaw 'Nuff – Dizzy Gillespie (1945)

Steeplechase – Charlie Parker (1948)

Straight Ahead – Kenny Dorham (1963)

The Theme – Miles Davis (1955)

Thriving On A Riff – Charlie Parker (1945)

Tippin' – Horace Silver (1956)